MOONSHINE MIXOLOGY

60 RECIPES

FOR FLAVORING SPIRITS & MAKING COCKTAILS

CORY STRAUB

STERLING EPICURE
New York

STERLING EPICURE
New York

STERLING EPICURE is a trademark of Sterling Publishing Co., Inc. The distinctive Sterling logo is a registered trademark of Sterling Publishing Co., Inc.

This book is intended as a source of information on the subject of distilling alcohol, a practice that, without proper compliance with national and local government regulations, is against the law in many countries, including America and Canada. The author and publisher of this book urge you to determine and follow all of your nation's laws in this regard. The author and publisher will not be held responsible for any claims, damages, or losses that may result from using information in this book in any way noncompliant with any and all applicable regulations.

ISBN 978-1-4549-2074-8

Distributed in Canada by Sterling Publishing Co., Inc.
c/o Canadian Manda Group, 664 Annette Street
Toronto, Ontario, M6S 2C8, Canada
Distributed in the United Kingdom by GMC Distribution Services
Castle Place, 166 High Street, Lewes, East Sussex, BN7 1XU, United Kingdom
Distributed in Australia by NewSouth Books
45 Beach Street, Coogee, NSW 2034, Australia

For information about custom editions, special sales, and premium and corporate purchases, please contact Sterling Special Sales at 800-805-5489 or specialsales@sterlingpublishing.com.

Manufactured in China

2 4 6 8 10 9 7 5 3 1

www.sterlingpublishing.com

To the memory of

ELAINE STRAUB

My strongest supporter and staunchest ally since the day I was born

CONTENTS

MOONSHINE MIXOLOGY

HISTORY
& HOW

HISTORY

In your hands you have the essential guide to mixing drinks with America's most notorious and often outlawed liquor—moonshine—also known as homebrew, hooch, mountain dew, white lightning, and white whiskey! People have been distilling this high-proof spirit since the late eighteenth century. Before we start making and mixing drinks, let's look at the history of this powerful liquid.

Many colonial farmers made moonshine. They did so to drink it, but they also made it to help get through a bad crop year or make use of excess grain. Long after the base ingredients would have gone bad, they could sell, trade, or barter moonshine for food, supplies, and seeds for the future. Some even used it to pay bills.

After the Revolutionary War, the new American government was swimming in debt and needed a way to raise money. The solution? Tax alcohol. Most farmers found the tax unfair and continued to make liquor covertly. They hid their

equipment and operated by the light of the moon—hence the term "moonshine." The government has gone after moonshiners ever since, with Kentucky, Virginia, and the Carolinas harboring the most offenders.

Public sentiment eventually soured, though, due to the onset of World War I and rising concern about the adverse effects of alcohol. With a variety of supporters, a truly national movement began in the early twentieth century and set out to ban alcohol altogether. Laws slowly curtailed alcohol sales and consumption. Then, in 1920, federal prohibition went into effect, but Prohibition totally backfired: Moonshiners loved it! Homebrewing and distilling skyrocketed, and the price of moonshine soared.

Moonshine became such a hot commodity that moonshiners couldn't keep up with the high demand. Distillers started using cheaper, more haphazard ingredients, sometimes even watering down their product. Countless speakeasies opened in nearly every city, and organized crime created empires from illegal distribution.

Prohibition failed to sober the nation and cost the federal and state governments billions in lost tax revenue. Its supporters fell to the wayside. The country repealed Prohibition in 1933, and the once enormous moonshine market crashed. But that didn't end the story. Moonshine continued to pose a problem well into the 1960s and 1970s. Many states revised their laws on home brewing and distilling over the course of the twentieth century, allowing intrepid home producers to rediscover this draught of American history—legally!—for themselves.

WHAT YOU NEED

If you want to create your own white lightning, you need a heat source, mash pot, cap with arm, thump keg (optional), worm box with fresh cold water available, a bucket or jar, and most importantly—a moonshine license. The basic ingredients are cornmeal, sugar, yeast, and water. Let's take a look at each of these in more detail.

Heat source: Use an open flame or fire, natural or propane gas flame, or electrical or steam heater that can reach 172° Fahrenheit. Eighteenth-century moonshiners used wood, coal, and steam, but your best option may be readily available propane.

Mash pot: This is where the moonshine ingredients ferment.

Cap with arm: This creates a sealed distilling system. Without a cap with arm, you'll lose alcohol content in the form of steam, and we don't want that!

Thump keg: This tool helps you achieve a higher concentration of distilled alcohol from the still the first time. It's a great time-saver.

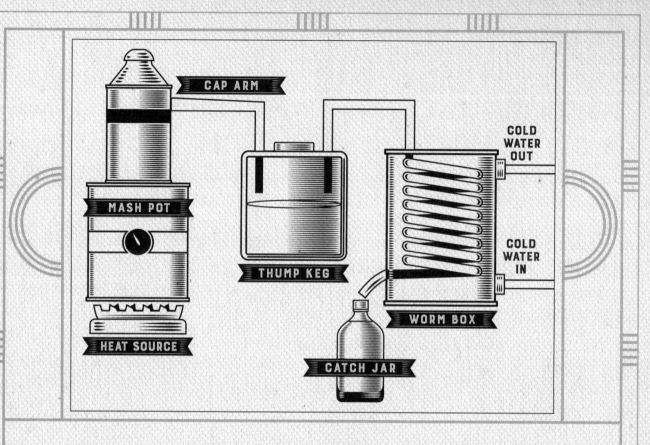

Worm box: The steam from the mash pot flows in the worm box—a long coil of copper inside a large barrel or tank—and then the fresh, cold water condenses the steam back into a liquid. Historically, the mash pot, cap with arm, and coil inside the worm box were made of copper to avoid adversely flavoring the alcohol and to ensure even heating. You can get the same results with stainless steel.

Moonshine license: To make moonshine legally, apply for a permit through the Alcohol and Tobacco Tax and Trade Bureau. Costs vary from state to state. For more information, visit *www.ttb.gov/spirits.*

Ingredients: If you're using whole kernels of corn, grind them first to release the starches that will act with the sugar and yeast to make the alcohol. If you use anything other than corn, technically you're not making moonshine. Some distillers use rye, barley, and certain types of rice. Some also use fruit, which will make the liquor taste more like brandy, or sugar cane, which will make it taste more like rum.

Use fine-ground sugar, which dissolves more quickly into the mash, and look for brewer's yeast. Several different types are available, so you might want to visit a brew supply store and ask a sales associate to help you pick out the best yeast for what you want to make. As for the water, the cleaner the better! Chlorine, for example, will kill the yeast and produce a poor product and low yield.

Maintenance: The equipment needs to be sanitized prior and after each use to prevent contamination. To clean it, use dish soap and hot water, or make your own cleaning solution by mixing ¼ cup of bleach with 1 gallon of water. Rinse thoroughly to remove flavor and odor.

HOW TO MAKE THE BASE MOONSHINE

Now that you have your equipment and ingredients, let's get started.

Grind 7 pounds of corn kernels into meal. Soak the cornmeal in enough hot water to completely cover it for 24 hours, then add 10 pounds of sugar. Pitch (add) yeast, and the fermentation process will begin within 24 to 48 hours. Now the ingredients are called mash. Once the alcohol level reaches the desired level—when the bubbling and gurgling slows or stops or a hydrometer measures a gravity around 1.4—transfer the mash to the mash pot of the still (if it's not already there), and slowly bring the mash temperature to about 172° F.

As the alcohol starts to evaporate, the alcohol steam will move up through the cap and arm and into the thump keg. The steam then goes into the worm, where it cools and condenses back into a liquid as the cold water circulates around the outside of the worm and into the filtered catch basin.

This recipe will produce between 1½ and 2 liters. When making moonshine, beware contamination. Always keep equipment as clean as possible; proper sanitation is crucial when making any kind of alcohol. Some moonshiners start with test batches to find a unique recipe that will set them apart from others, but be careful; you may wind up with a batch that can make you sick. Use food-grade ingredients and equipment, and always follow proper procedures to avoid bad tastes and bellyaches.

If you don't have the equipment, ingredients, or a proper license, don't fret—you can still make delicious white lightning cocktails. Just buy plain moonshine at your local liquor store.

MOONSHINE MIXOLOGY

FLAVORING

TASTY FLAVORS

Most pure moonshine is darn difficult to swallow, but it doesn't have to be!

First I tried hiding its harshness in mixed drinks, but that raw edge still came through the mixers. Candy flavoring oils didn't work either. The oils didn't mix, and they tasted even more poignant than the moonshine!

Fruit and fresh herbs worked OK, but with a few caveats: limited availability of ingredients and the time it took for the flavor to stick. If you use only fruit and herbs, allocate lots of time for extracting the flavors.

Baking extracts worked well. You can add them days or even weeks before, or while mixing a drink with the same swoon-worthy results.

Here are sixteen successful ways to flavor moonshine that call for extracts, herbs, fruit, and seasonings. These guidelines will get you started, but play around and see what you like. I prefer my flavor strong, so you might want to halve the amounts, try a taste, and adjust from there. Remember, it's all about having fun and making unique hooch for you and your friends. If something sounds tasty, give it a go, and see how it turns out.

If you buy base moonshine, sample different brands; flavors vary far and wide from one manufacturer to the next.

ALMOND

EXTRACT FLAVOR

Pour 1 teaspoon of almond extract into a fifth of moonshine, and swirl. This amount will add a subtle almond flavor to the liquor, so the burn may still shine through. Add a few more drops to soften it if you like.

APRICOT

NATURAL FLAVOR

Chop up 8 ounces of dried apricots into small pieces and add to a fifth of moonshine. They'll give the liquor a golden color and great flavor. You can strain out the apricots or leave them in to embellish the booze.

CINNAMON

NATURAL FLAVOR

Put 2 whole cinnamon sticks in a fifth of moonshine for a week to brew a mighty cinnamon flavor. Your friends will love the strong yet sweet spiciness. If you want less spice, remove the sticks after a few days.

COCONUT

EXTRACT FLAVOR

Pouring 1 teaspoon of coconut extract into a fifth of moonshine produces a strong but smooth coconut taste. To tame down the nuttiness, use ½ teaspoon. Enjoy this shine in tropical drinks.

COFFEE

NATURAL FLAVOR

Here are two delicious, full-bodied options.

1) Put 1 teaspoon of coffee grounds in a tea ball, and let it sit in 3 ounces of moonshine. It will infuse well, but the grounds may seep from the tea ball into the liquid.

2) Brew coffee in a French press, and add 2 ounces of it to 3 ounces of moonshine.

CRANBERRY

NATURAL FLAVOR

Chop up 4 ounces of dried cranberries and add them to a fifth of moonshine. After a week, the moonshine will take on a great crimson color and refreshing flavor. Leave the cranberries in the liquor for a little kick while you sip!

GINGER

NATURAL FLAVOR

At the grocery store look for fresh ginger that's pre-sliced into ⅛-inch slices. Soak 16 slices in a fifth of moonshine for a week. Muddle it a bit throughout the week to release more of the warm, spicy taste.

JALAPEÑO

NATURAL FLAVOR

Use this recipe for a double burn! Cut a whole jalapeño into 16 slices; leave the seeds or remove a few, depending on how hot you want the hooch. Put the slices in a fifth of moonshine, and let it sit for at least a week. Test it with a chaser in hand since it will be warm. Enjoy the flavoring alongside a Mexican dinner—think fajitas—or try mixing a bit into your dish while cooking for a little extra kick!

LEMON

EXTRACT FLAVOR

Lemon will blunt the burn
while leaving a satisfying citrus
aftertaste. Pour 1 teaspoon of
lemon extract into a fifth of
moonshine and swirl. Place a
lemon twist or slice inside for
a little extra zing.

MAPLE

EXTRACT FLAVOR

This mouth-warming flavor rivals any maple whiskey, and you can use it to mix a hot toddy that goes down nice and smooth. Pour 1 teaspoon of maple extract into a fifth of moonshine, and give it a swirl.

MINT

NATURAL FLAVOR

This refreshing mint mixture is one of my favorite flavorings. To make, dice ¾ ounce of spearmint leaves, place it in cheese cloth or an infusion pouch, and combine with a fifth of moonshine; let that sit for a week to soak up a cool, crisp taste.

ORANGE

EXTRACT FLAVOR

The evident orange in this mixture will charm your taste buds and your nose. The citrus cuts through the burn and creates a very drinkable spirit. Pour 1 teaspoon of orange extract into a fifth of moonshine and swirl. Add a couple of orange slices for extra flavor.

RASPBERRY

EXTRACT FLAVOR

Pour 1 teaspoon of raspberry extract into a fifth of moonshine and swirl. Add a small handful of whole raspberries for a little extra flavor and color. This sweet-and-sour shine is tasty as a mixer or by itself on the rocks.

ROOT BEER

EXTRACT FLAVOR

There's no sugar in this flavor base, so it won't taste sweet, but the flavor is perfect for your next adult root beer float. To mix, pour 1 teaspoon of root beer extract into a fifth of moonshine and swirl.

SWEET TEA

NATURAL FLAVOR

Place 1 tea bag in a double shot of moonshine (3 ounces), and let it steep for 24 hours. Add 1 teaspoon of sugar. You'll certainly taste sweet tea, but beware of the stealthy burn.

VANILLA

NATURAL FLAVOR

For a mellow, easy-to-drink base for flavorful hair-of-the-dog cocktails, drop 4 whole vanilla pods into a fifth of moonshine, and let them steep for 2 weeks.

MOONSHINE MIXOLOGY

COCKTAILS

ANGRY APPLE

Grandma's apple pie never tasted so good . . . and it never made you feel tipsy either!

2 ounces sour apple schnapps
1½ ounces plain moonshine
dash apple juice
ginger ale
apple for garnish

Combine and stir liquid ingredients in a mason jar or highball glass with crushed ice. Garnish with apple slices and an optional cinnamon stick.

VARIATION

Rub the rim of a shot glass with an apple slice and dip it into a mixture of cinnamon and sugar. Pour 1 ounce plain moonshine and 1 ounce sour apple schnapps into the shot glass.

APRICOT MOON

This little number is light and refreshing, and it's perfect for a long, lazy summer evening with friends.

> **2 ounces apricot moonshine (p. 23)**
> **½ ounce grenadine**
> **½ ounce fresh lemon juice**
> **lemon-lime soda**
> **apricot for garnish**
> **lemon for garnish**

Pour liquid ingredients into a Collins glass over ice. Garnish with apricot slices and a lemon wheel.

VARIATION

Transform this cocktail into a shot by pouring 1½ ounces apricot moonshine and ½ ounce grenadine into a chilled shot glass. Drink up!

BANANA BANSHEE

Pack your smoothie with a punch! You won't taste much of the moonshine in this drink, but it will have you howling for more.

2 ounces almond moonshine (p. 22)
½ ounce Irish cream liqueur
6–8 ounces almond milk
½ banana
banana for garnish

Blend the first four ingredients with ice until smooth. Pour into a chilled martini glass and garnish with banana slices.

VARIATION

For a low-calorie version of the Banana Banshee, substitute skim milk for the almond milk. It keeps the creaminess but cuts the calories.

BELLA LUNA

Tired of the same old boring mimosas weeked after weekend? Want something a little more exciting and with more depth of flavor? Try this recipe, which serves eight, so you can share it with your nearest and dearest. Rise and shine!

1 peach
1 cup sliced strawberries
24 basil leaves, plus 8 for garnish
½ cup sugar
juice of 2 limes
1½ cups vanilla moonshine (p. 37)
1 bottle sparkling wine
1 liter sparkling water

Muddle peach, strawberries, 24 basil leaves, and sugar in a large shaker. Add ice, lime juice, and moonshine, then shake until cold. Evenly pour mixture into eight chilled highball glasses and fill with equal parts sparkling wine and sparkling water. Garnish with basil leaves.

FUN FACT

Other than hiding moonshine in their boots, bootleggers held fake funerals and filled the coffins with larger shipments of moonshine.

BLOODY SHINER

Kick-start your brunch with this eye-opening concoction. Nothing will wake you up and get you going more quickly than some heat, spice, and moonshine on ice.

> 2 ounces plain moonshine
> 2 ounces pilsner beer
> Bloody Mary mix
> dash pickle juice
> juice of 1 lime
> salt and pepper to taste
> celery stalk for garish
> pickle spear for garnish
> crispy bacon strip for garnish
> 3 green olives for garnish

Pour moonshine and beer over ice in a mason jar and add Bloody Mary mix (tomato juice, lemon juice, lime juice, horseradish, Worcestershire sauce, garlic, and hot sauce if you want to make your own). Add a dash of pickle juice and lime juice, and season to taste. Add garnishes.

TIP

Get creative with your garnishes; something salty, crunchy, or sour tastes best. Keep adding and you can turn this savory drink into a meal.

CHEEKY CRANBERRY

This sensuous spirit is sure to delight your taste buds. Cranberry, vermouth, and amaretto were made to share a glass.

- **1 ounce cranberry moonshine (p. 27)**
- **1 ounce sweet vermouth**
- **½ ounce amaretto**
- **lemonade**
- **cranberries for garnish**
- **orange for garnish**

Shake moonshine, vermouth, and amaretto with ice in a shaker until cold. Place a few ice cubes in a highball glass and pour the mixture on top. Fill the rest of the glass with lemonade, and garnish with cranberries and an orange twist.

TIP

Depending on the time of year, it may be difficult to find fresh cranberries, but you can always purchase them from the freezer section of your grocery store. Add the frozen berries to your cocktails to keep your drinks cool without watering them down.

CITRUS SMASH

Serve your taste buds something new with this lip-smacking blend of citrus and apricot. The subtlety and sweetness of the apricot mildly balances the sourness of the puckery lemon and lime.

> **2 ounces apricot moonshine (p. 23)**
> **1 ounce lemon moonshine (p. 30)**
> **juice of 1 lime**
> **club soda**
> **lemon for garnish**
> **lime for garnish**

Pour moonshines and lime juice into a Collins glass with ice. Fill with club soda and stir. Garnish with thin lemon and lime slices.

TIP

To add some extra sweetness to the recipe, swap out the club soda for your favorite lemon-lime soda.

COCONUT RAZZMATAZZ

Treat your taste buds to something tropical with the Coconut Razzmatazz. This delicious drink is vacation in a glass.

> **2 ounces coconut moonshine (p. 25)**
> **2 ounces raspberry schnapps**
> **½ ounce coconut rum**
> **juice of 1 lime**
> **lemon-lime soda**
> **raspberries for garnish**

Mix the first four ingredients in a mason jar or highball glass. Add ice and enough lemon-lime soda to fill the glass. Float raspberries on top.

FUN FACT

Moonshine is called "white lightning" because plain moonshine has no color.

CRAN IN THE MOON

Kick up your feet and savor the flavor of this clean, light-bodied sipper. It tastes like summer in a glass, but it's prefect for surviving Thanksgiving with the family.

> 2 ounces cranberry moonshine (p. 27)
> 4 ounces cranberry juice
> 2 ounces ginger ale
> cranberries for garnish

Add all ingredients to a shaker with ice and shake until cold. Pour the mixture into a highball glass and garnish with cranberries.

VARIATION

Make a lighter version of this drink by using light cranberry juice and diet ginger ale. You'll enjoy the same delicious flavors with less sugar and fewer calories.

DAIQUIRI SHINE

Add some class to your glass with this cocktail. Then brighten it up with freshly cut slices of pineapple and lime.

   2 ounces plain moonshine
   2 ounces pineapple juice
   ½ ounce simple syrup
   juice of 1 lime
   lime slice for garnish
   pineapple for garnish

Shake the first four ingredients in a shaker with ice until cold. Pour into a chilled highball glass and garnish with a lime wheel and pineapple slice.

VARIATION

Use a blender instead of a shaker to make a thicker, cooler drink.

FULL MOON DALY

Everyone knows that an Arnold Palmer is iced tea and lemonade, but if you add vodka you get a John Daly (another pro golfer). This twist on that drink packs a heavy punch, but one sip will transport you down south.

> 2 ounces sweet tea moonshine (p. 36)
> 1 ounce lemon juice
> 1 teaspoon sugar
> iced tea
> lemon for garnish

Mix moonshine, lemon juice, and sugar, and pour into a Collins or hurricane glass over ice. Fill with iced tea, and garnish with lemon slices and a lemon twist.

VARIATION

Add 1 ounce lemon moonshine (p. 30) to make the tea stronger; it will enhance the lemon and give you that added punch you're looking for. Add more sugar if you prefer sweeter tea.

GRAPE NUMBER 5

Named for its five ingredients, this grape drink will make you nostalgic for your childhood, but this one has a little something extra. Try it with red or white grape juice.

2 ounces plain moonshine
2 ounces grape juice
1 ounce grenadine
splash lime juice
6–8 ounces lemon-lime soda
lime for garnish

Pour liquid ingredients into a highball glass over ice, stir well, and garnish with a lime twist and lime slices, or, for the ultimate throwback, garnish with some Bootleg Bears (p. 133).

NOT SO FUN FACT

During Prohibition, some moonshiners added ingredients to their moonshine to make it stand out from the rest, but some of the additives were questionable at best: paint thinner, bleach, embalming fluid, and even manure! Unfortunately these "modifiers" often caused blindness, paralysis, and even death.

HARVEST MOON

As the days grow shorter and the nights grow colder, cozy up on your couch with this versatile cocktail. It tastes like fall in a cup and will warm you up however you make it.

> 2 ounces plain moonshine
> 1 cup apple cider
> cinnamon stick for garnish
> apple for garnish

Add moonshine to hot, cold, or sparkling apple cider, and garnish with a cinnamon stick. For hot cider, use an Irish coffee cup; for cold cider, use a chilled cocktail glass; and for sparkling cider, a Champagne flute. Sprinkle an apple wheel with cinnamon and place it on the rim.

TIP

For best results, don't use powdered cider mix. Add in 1 ounce cinnamon moonshine (p. 24) for a stronger, spicier version.

JALAPEÑO MOONARITA

A shiner margarita with a jalapeño kick! The agave nectar balances out the spice but leaves you with just enough heat to satisfy your hankering for a hot drink.

1 lime wedge
kosher salt
4 ounces jalapeño moonshine (p. 29)
2 ounces triple sec
juice of 2 limes
1 tablespoon agave nectar
lime for garnish
jalapeño for garnish

Rim a rocks glass or margarita glass with a lime wedge. Dip the rim into a plate of salt to coat it. Fill the glass with ice and set aside. Pour jalapeño moonshine, triple sec, lime juice, and agave nectar into a shaker with ice and shake until cold. Strain into the prepared glass and garnish with a lime wheel and jalapeño slices.

VARIATION

Make it a shooter by rimming a shot glass with salt. Add 1½ ounces jalapeño moonshine and ½ ounce triple sec. Perfect for your next Cinco de Mayo party!

LEMON MOONADE

This cocktail will make your lips pucker! Drink it as is, or lighten it up with a bit of sugar.

> 1 ounce lemon moonshine (p. 30)
> 1 ounce triple sec
> 3 ounces lemonade
> dash lemon-lime soda
> lemon for garnish

Pour liquid ingredients over ice in a shaker and shake well. Strain the chilled mixture into a mason jar or highball glass and garnish with a lemon twist and slices.

TIP

Add some citrus to your drink with a lemon twist garnish. Make it by carefully removing a thin layer of lemon peel using a Y-shaped vegetable peeler or sharp knife. Peel as little of the pith as possible.

LUNARITA

You're going to love this moonshine take on the traditional Margarita. Try it on May 5—or any other time.

> ¼ cup kosher salt
> 2 ounces plain moonshine
> ½ ounce triple sec
> juice of 1 lime
> lime for garnish

Rub lime wedge around rim of rocks glass. Dip rim into a plate of salt to coat it, and set aside. Add remaining ingredients to shaker with ice and shake well. Fill the glass with ice and strain the mixture into a glass. Garnish with lime slices.

VARIATION

A proper Margarita isn't frozen, but that shouldn't stop you from enjoying it that way if that's how you like it. Blend the ingredients with ice, then pour into a margarita glass.

MINT SHINE COLLINS

This is a simple recipe, but it taste like sophistication at its finest. Make this cool, crisp cocktail the next time you want to cool off and impress your friends.

2 ounces mint moonshine (p. 32)
juice of 1 lemon
club soda
lemon for garnish
orange for garnish
cherry for garnish
1 sprig mint for garnish

Shake the moonshine and lemon juice over ice in a shaker and strain into a Collins glass over ice. Fill with club soda and stir gently. Add garnishes.

VARIATION

Add a splash of your favorite beer instead of the soda water. The beer will balance the mint and retain the mouth-tingling fizz.

MOON OVER MY CHERRIES

This simple take on sweet and sour is delicious and divine. Its assertive taste will take you to the moon and back.

> 2 ounces plain moonshine
> 2 ounces cherry juice
> ¼ ounce grenadine
> dash lemon juice
> Cherry Bombs for garnish (p. 136)
> lemon slice for garnish

Shake the liquid ingredients together in a shaker with ice. Strain the mixture into a chilled rocks glass and garnish with Cherry Bombs and a lemon wheel.

VARIATION

To add another level of flavor to this concoction, substitute the plain moonshine with orange moonshine.

MOONHATTAN

This is a down-home take on a classic cocktail that evokes New York City in the Gilded Age. The recipe is simple, but the bitters make it taste a bit more complex.

2 ounces plain moonshine
1 ounce sweet vermouth
dash bitters
lemon for garnish
cocktail cherries for garnish

Shake the liquid ingredients over ice until cold. Rub lemon peel around the rim of a chilled martini glass. Strain the mixture into a glass and garnish with a lemon twist and cherries.

FUN FACT

During Prohibition, alcohol consumption soared to record levels.

MOONING THE BEACH

One sip of this special summer cocktail and you'll feel the ocean breeze blowing.
It will transport you straight to the beach! Make this drink for your next summer
barbecue or a tropical stay-cation.

> 1 ounce coconut moonshine (p. 25)
> ½ ounce almond moonshine (p. 22)
> 4 ounces orange juice
> ½ ounce grenadine
> orange for garnish

Shake moonshines and orange juice in a shaker filled with ice until cold.
Strain into a glass, with ice if desired. Add grenadine, stir, and garnish
with an orange wheel.

FUN FACT

When Prohibition put the kibosh on stateside drinking, cocktail culture sailed
east to Europe and south to the Caribbean, where bartenders made use of local
ingredients and eventually kicked off the tiki craze.

MOONJITO

Put a twist on one of the world's most popular cocktails with this recipe. You'll still get that minty, cooling taste—but with a bigger kick!

6 mint leaves, plus 1 sprig for garnish
2 teaspoons sugar
juice of 1 lime
1½ ounces plain moonshine
club soda

Muddle mint leaves with sugar and juice in the bottom of a Collins glass. Add ice and moonshine. Add enough club soda to fill the glass and stir gently. Garnish with the mint sprig and serve with a straw.

FUN FACT

Ever wonder where the term "moonshine" comes from? When the making of liquor was taxed or declared illegal, distillers who continued making it did so out of sight and during the night—by the light of the moon. It's an old British term that stuck in America.

MOONLIGHT JULEP

Can't make it to Churchill Downs in Louisville for Derby Day? Let your mixology skills take you there with this cocktail. The light, refreshing taste will put you in the perfect mood to watch the races.

4 sprigs mint
2 teaspoons sugar
2 teaspoons cold water
1 teaspoon powdered sugar
2 ounces mint moonshine (p. 32)

Muddle 3 mint springs, sugar, and water in a sliver julep cup. Fill with crushed ice and add moonshine. Top off with more ice and garnish with a mint sprig.

FUN FACT

The difference between moonshine and whiskey is that moonshine isn't aged at all, and whiskey ages for at least five years, usually in charred white oak barrels that impart its distinctive color.

MOONLITE MILE

This drink is delicious during hot summer days. Make it even more refreshing by preparing fresh watermelon juice (p. 101).

2 ounces plain moonshine
2 ounces watermelon juice
diet tonic water
watermelon for garnish

Pour moonshine and watermelon juice into a mason jar or highball glass over ice. Fill the glass with tonic and garnish with a slice of fresh watermelon.

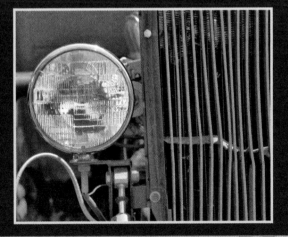

FUN FACT

During Prohibition, some intrepid distillers used car radiators to make moonshine. Many radiators had traces of antifreeze, containing the very poisonous ethylene glycol, and usually were soldered together with lead, which caused lead poisoning. Drinker beware!

MOONRISE

This is a great recipe to add to your mixologist repertoire. You need only three ingredients to whip up this swanky cocktail. Serve some up at your next brunch or as a summer afternoon indulgence.

2 ounces cranberry moonshine (p. 27)
orange juice
cranberries for garnish
orange for garnish

Pour cranberry moonshine into a chilled rocks glass, and fill the rest of the glass with orange juice and stir. Add cranberries and an orange slice to garnish. You can also serve this cocktail on the rocks if you like.

TIP

Always use fresh-squeezed juices to make drinks tastier and more lively.

MOONSHINE HEAVEN

This complex cocktail boasts divine flavors balanced in perfect harmony. Pour yourself a glass of paradise, and treat yourself to a wedge of heaven.

> 1¼ ounces plain moonshine
> ¾ ounce almond moonshine (p. 22)
> ¾ ounce raspberry moonshine (p. 34)
> splash cranberry juice
> splash pineapple juice
> raspberries for garnish
> pineapple for garnish

Put all ingredients into a shaker with ice and shake until cold. Strain into a Collins glass over ice and stir. Garnish with a pineapple wedge and raspberries.

"We are here, and it is now. Further than that, all human knowledge is moonshine."
—H. L. Mencken

MOSCOW MOON

This variation of a Moscow Mule has added kick. Serve it in a copper mug to keep the drink authentic, the flavor intact, and the temperature just right.

8 ounces ginger beer
2 ounces ginger moonshine (p. 28)
juice of 2 limes
lime for garnish

Combine the liquid ingredients over ice in a copper mug and stir gently. Garnish with a lime wheel and enjoy.

FUN FACT

Bootleggers built their cars to outrun the law. Some of them got together and created racetracks for their cars, which eventually turned into NASCAR.

ORANGE CRESCENT

Put your feet up and get comfortable before indulging in this dreamsicle of a drink that will treat your sense of smell as well as your taste buds.

2 ounces almond moonshine (p. 22)
2 ounces apricot moonshine (p. 23)
orange juice
2 ounces heavy whipping cream or half and half
orange for garnish

Combine moonshines in a Collins glass with ice. Fill with fresh orange juice, leaving room for the cream. Add cream, stir, and garnish with an orange wheel.

VARIATION

Blend the ingredients for a desert smoothie with kick.

PINEAPPLE GINGER ECLIPSE

The combination of ginger and pineapple make this cocktail pop! Be careful, though, this fun and bright drink goes down really smooth.

2 ounces ginger moonshine (p. 28)
2 ounces pineapple juice
1 ounce fruit punch
ginger ale
pineapple for garnish

Mix the first three ingredients in a mason jar or highball glass. Add ginger ale and ice. Garnish with a pineapple wedge.

VARIATION

Pineapple cocktails are perfect for parties. With this one you easily can increase the amounts to make a big batch in a punch bowl. Set out a bowl of ice and pineapple slices so your guests can pour and garnish their own drinks.

2 cups ginger moonshine (p. 28)
3 cups pineapple juice
2 cups fruit punch
1 cup ginger ale
pineapple for garnish

POMEGRANATE SHINER

The tang of the pomegranate juice blends beautifully with the burn of white whiskey in this stylish cocktail that would feel right at home at a swanky speakeasy or lounge.

    1 lime wedge
    kosher salt
    4 ounces plain moonshine
    2 ounces triple sec
    4 ounces pomegranate juice
    juice of 1 lime
    club soda
    1 lime for garnish

Rub 1 lime wedge around the rim of the chilled mason jar or highball glass. Dip the glass into a plate of salt to coat it. Fill the glass with ice and set aside. Shake the moonshine, triple sec, pomegranate juice, and lime juice in a shaker with ice until cold. Pour the mixture into the salt-rimmed glass and fill with club soda. Garnish with a lime slice.

FUN FACT

Before Prohibition, some towns sold their jails because they thought that without alcohol there was no need for them.

RAZZ & SHINE

This cocktail flaunts a juicy flavor medley of fruits perfect for brunch or as an indulgent dessert. The sweet, tart tastes creates a refreshing complexity and will make your mouth water for more.

    8 raspberries
    ¼ teaspoon sugar
    4 ice cubes
    2 ounces raspberry moonshine (p. 34)
    2 ounces cranberry juice
    2 ounces orange juice
    club soda
    lime for garnish

Muddle 3 raspberries and sugar in the bottom of a Collins glass. Add ice. Pour moonshine and juices over the ice. Fill with club soda. Garnish with the remaining raspberries and a lime slice.

VARIATION

For a session-strength version, reduce the moonshine to 1 ounce. It's still a tasty sipper, but it won't pack quite as big of a punch.

RED MOON RISING

Serve this drink at your next Fourth of July or Memorial Day party. Make your own watermelon juice for an extra-fresh American Red Moon Rising.

2 ounces plain moonshine
½ ounce triple sec
2 ounces watermelon juice
½ ounce lemon juice
lemon-lime soda
watermelon for garnish
lemon for garnish

Pour the first four ingredients into a shaker and shake with ice. Strain the mixture into a chilled rocks glass. Fill the rest of the glass with lemon-lime soda. Garnish with a watermelon slice and lemon wheel.

TIP

It's so easy to make fresh watermelon juice. Mash or juice a watermelon and strain. That's it!

ROOT BEER SINK OR SWIM

Say hello to the adult take on the traditional root beer float. The Irish cream and flavored moonshine make this ode to childhood a bit more interesting and surprisingly sweet.

> **2 ounces root beer moonshine (p. 35)**
> **1 ounce Irish cream liqueur**
> **6–8 ounces root beer**
> **1 scoop vanilla ice cream**

Pour the moonshine, Irish cream, and root beer in a footed pilsner or other large glass and mix them together. Add a scoop of ice cream on top, and enjoy.

TIP

Sprinkle cinnamon on top of your float to take the presentation up a notch and add more depth of flavor.

SEX ON THE MOON

Here's your moonshiner version of Sex on the Beach. This fruit-forward cocktail will put you in the mood and take you out of this world.

- 3 strawberries
- 2 teaspoons sugar
- 1½ ounces plain moonshine
- ½ ounce peach schnapps
- 2 ounces cranberry juice
- 2 ounces orange juice
- orange for garnish

Muddle strawberries with sugar in a shaker, then add the moonshine, schnapps, and juices, and shake well over ice. Strain the mixture into a highball glass over ice and garnish with an orange slice.

TIP

Why muddle? Muddling herbs, fruit, or vegetables releases a stronger flavor. If you don't have a muddler, you can use a large spoon instead.

SHINY GINGER

If you love ginger, this drink is right up your alley. Go easy on the lemon juice to savor the full flavor of ginger and achieve more zest and spice.

2 ounces ginger moonshine (p. 28)
6–8 ounces ginger ale
dash lemon juice
lemon for garnish

Pour the moonshine and ginger ale together over ice in a rocks glass. Add a dash of lemon juice and a lemon twist.

FUN FACT

George Washington had red hair as a younger man. He also was one of the most prominent moonshiners in colonial times. He built a distillery on his Mount Vernon estate!

SHOOT THE BANANA

This shooter packs a lot of flavor in a small punch. It's sweet but strong. Make a batch for your next party with friends.

    1 tablespoon sugar
    1 teaspoon cinnamon
    1½ ounces vanilla moonshine (p. 37)
    1 ounce banana liqueur

Rim the shot glass with a mixture of sugar and cinnamon and set aside. Pour the moonshine and banana liqueur into a shaker with ice and shake until cold. Strain the mixture into the glass and knock it back. Also try it with a candy shot glass (p. 134)

VARIATION

Turn this recipe into a more sophisticated cocktail by pouring liquid ingredients into a Collins glass with ice. Add ½ ounce simple syrup and fill with club soda.

SILVER BULLET

So simple and so classy, this one is a winner for any occasion. There's not much to crafting this cocktail, but the clean and simple flavors make this drink shine.

- 1 ounce lemon moonshine (p. 30)
- 1 ounce plain moonshine
- 8 ounces lemon-lime soda
- lime for garnish

Pour lemon moonshine and plain moonshine over ice in a rocks glass. Top with lemon-lime soda, stir gently, and garnish with a lime wheel.

FUN FACT

Rumrunners transported alcohol by boat rather than by land.

SPARKLING RAZZ

Look to this elegant spritzer to elevate your next party. It's as tasty as it is beautiful to behold, and it raises moonshine cocktails to a higher plane. Cheers!

1 ounce raspberry moonshine (p. 34)
2 ounces lemonade
splash lime juice
sparkling wine
raspberries for garnish

Pour the raspberry moonshine and lemonade into a flute. Add a splash of lime juice. Fill with sparkling wine and garnish with raspberries.

TIP

Try a variety of sparkling wines for this cocktail. Use a sparkling dessert wine for guests who prefer a sweeter spritzer, and have a brut on hand for those who like drier drinks.

SPICY MOON

Wake up your taste buds with this surprising twist on a traditional cocktail. As soon as you feel the heat from the jalapeño, the soothing flavors of mint, ginger, and lime emerge to cool your palate.

- 2 mint leaves, plus 1 sprig for garnish
- ¼ teaspoon sugar
- 1½ ounces jalapeño moonshine (p. 29)
- juice of 1 lime
- ginger beer
- jalapeño for garnish
- lime for garnish

Muddle the mint leaves and sugar in the bottom of a mason jar or highball glass. Add ice, jalapeño moonshine, and lime juice. Fill with ginger beer, and garnish with a jalapeño slice, lime wheel, and mint sprig.

TIP

Always use fresh-squeezed lime juice—never the stuff from a store-bought green plastic bottle. Freshness is key to any cocktail. Use a lime slicer to make cutting and measuring easier.

STRAWBERRY SHINER

Serve this sweet, sour, and sexy Strawberry Shiner with chocolate-covered strawberries on a romantic evening.

> 4 strawberries
> 2¼ teaspoons sugar
> 2 ounces plain moonshine
> 2 ounces sweet and sour mix
> dash lemon juice
> lemon for garnish

Muddle the strawberries in a shaker with 2 teaspoons of sugar. Add the moonshine, sweet and sour mix, lemon juice, and remaining sugar. Shake with ice and pour into a chilled highball glass. Garnish with a lemon twist.

FUN FACT

The "XXX" on a bottle of moonshine lets you know that it's legitimate. Three "X"s signifies it was run through the still three times, which means it's almost pure alcohol.

TROPICAL SHINE

One sip of this tiki concoction will transport you to paradise. Make it your go-to for a hot summer day and rejuvenate your spirits with this beautiful blend of flavors. Close your eyes, relax, and sip this one nice and easy.

> 3 ounces coconut moonshine (p. 25)
> 6 ounces pineapple juice
> 1 ounce cranberry juice
> splash lemon-lime soda
> lime for garnish
> pineapple for garnish

Fill a highball or Collins glass with ice. Add moonshine and juices. Top with a splash of lemon-lime soda and stir well. Add thinly sliced wheels of lime and garnish with a lime wheel and pineapple wedge.

TIP

Upgrade your presentation with fun and funky straws. The extra pop of color will brighten colorful cocktails even that much more.

VANILLA VIXEN

The simple and soothing scents of vanilla and cinnamon will help you ease into the night, so sit back, relax, and sip this vixen under the light of the moon.

1½ ounces vanilla moonshine (p. 37)
1 ounce cinnamon moonshine (p. 24)
cola

Pour the moonshines over ice into a rocks glass. Fill with cola, stir gently, and serve with a straw.

VARIATION

For a Havana version of this drink, add the juice of 1 lime for a Luna Libre.

WEREWOLF

Grapefruit has the right combination of sweet and sour to stand up to the kick of the moonshine in this drink. Its strong citrus flavor is ideal for drinking during warmer months when you want to howl at the moon.

2 ounces plain moonshine
4 ounces grapefruit juice
grapefruit for garnish

Pour the moonshine and juice into a Collins glass over ice. Stir well and garnish with a grapefruit wedge.

VARIATION

Make a Salty Wolf by adding salt around the rim, which creates a whole new flavor profile. To punch it up more, use 2 ounces of jalapeño moonshine (p. 29) instead of plain shine and garnish with a jalapeño slice. The salt and spice will balance the tart grapefruit.

WHITE WHISKEY RUSSIAN

This creamy cocktail is perfect for when it feels like a Russian winter outside. Savor it as is or sweeten it, dessert-style, with a squirt of chocolate syrup.

1½ ounces plain moonshine
½ ounce coffee liqueur
milk
coffee beans for garnish
cinnamon stick for garnish

Pour the moonshine and coffee liqueur into a rocks glass over ice. Fill with milk and stir slowly to mix. Garnish with coffee beans and a cinnamon stick.

VARIATION

For an even sweeter, creamier consistency, add ½ ounce of half and half or your favorite coffee creamer.

WINE & SHINE SANGRIA

Share this shiny take on the Spanish punch with friends and family over a weekend breakfast or brunch. The twelve grapes are for good luck, so divide them evenly if you can. Serves four to six. *Salud!*

> 1 bottle dry red wine
> ½ gallon orange juice (no pulp)
> 1 cup cranberry moonshine (p. 27)
> 4 ounces triple sec
> juice of 1 lime
> 20 strawberries, sliced
> 2 oranges, segmented
> 12 grapes
> 1 two-liter bottle ginger ale

Pour all the ingredients except ginger ale into a large pitcher or bowl. Refrigerate for at least 2 hours or overnight. Add the ginger ale before serving.

TIP

Keep your sangria cold without watering it down by using frozen fruit. If you want to dilute the mixture a little for longer drinking, freeze fruit inside ice cubes and drop them in the ginger ale.

MOONSHINE MIXOLOGY

PARTY ON

TREATS & GIFTS

Now that you know how to make, flavor, and mix a collection of delicious moonshine cocktails, let's celebrate all things 'shine even more with fun party treats and gifting ideas. Here's what you need to know to put together unique party ideas and décor, dress up drinks for booze-loving friends and family, and store white whiskey—all of which you can do easily in the comfort of your own bar or kitchen. As a gift, alcohol may prove short-lived, but it won't be forgotten if it's heartfelt and thoughtfully given.

BOOTLEG BEARS

Grown-up gummy candies are great for parties and require only a few simple steps. You also can use them as fun colorful garnishes—in the Grape Number 5 (p. 62) for example.

1 bag gummy candies
plain or flavored moonshine

Put gummies in a bowl and pour moonshine over them until the moonshine covers the gummies by ¾ inch. Place the bowl, covered or uncovered, in the fridge for 5–6 days, stirring daily, before serving.

TIP

If you want to serve them as a party treat, set out a plate of toothpicks for easy eating.

CANDY SHOT GLASSES

If you make high-quality moonshine, your guests won't mind how you serve it, so go big with these small candy shot glasses. Cook down hard candies that complement the flavors of the moonshine you're serving and keep the glasses chilled so the shot goes down nice and easy.

hard fruit candies

Preheat oven to 350°F. Fill oven-safe silicone shot glass molds with hard candies. Place the mold on a baking sheet and bake until candies melt, about 10–15 minutes. Remove from the oven and let cool. Refrigerate the shot glasses for 2–3 days until completely hardened, then carefully remove them from the mold. Return the shot glasses to the refrigerator or freezer until ready to use.

TIP

Use different flavored candies to create colored and multicolored shot glasses.

CHERRY BOMBS

These alcohol-infused fruit explosions are great to pop in your mouth or use as a garnish for your favorite drinks. You also can soak strawberries, mangoes, watermelon, or pineapple with this recipe. The sweetness will mask the harshness of the moonshine while creating a refreshing treat.

16 ounces plain moonshine
15–20 maraschino cherries

Drop the cherries into a mason jar and fill with moonshine. Seal the jar and keep it in the refrigerator for between a week and 30 days to let the moonshine really soak in.

FUN FACT

The "high end" or "head" are the first few ounces of moonshine made in a batch.

CHOCOLATE CHERRY BOMBS

Make your moonshine cherries more indulgent with a dark chocolate coating and crushed candy toppings.

>   2 (10-ounce) bags dark chocolate chips
>   Cherry Bombs (p. 136)
>   crushed candies (optional)

Microwave dark chocolate chips in a microwave-safe bowl for 1 minute. Remove from the microwave and stir. Repeat, heating in 15–20 second intervals, stirring in between, until the chocolate completely melts. Dip Cherry Bombs into the chocolate a few at a time until fully coated, then place on a sheet of parchment paper to cool. Add crushed candy toppings. Arrange on a plate or platter.

TIP

Use milk or white chocolate as well, and add drizzles on larger fruit pieces.

MOONSHINE CANDY POPS

These crushed candy lollipops make great gifts or garnishes for your drinks. Make them in bulk because they won't last long.

- 1 bag rock candy
- 2 ounces plain moonshine,
  plus 1 tablespoon
- 2 tablespoons water
- ¾ cup granulated sugar
- 3 tablespoons corn syrup
- pinch of salt

Crush rock candy and place it on a silicon mat in small piles or in lollipop molds. Add moonshine, water, sugar, corn syrup, and salt to a saucepan and bring to a boil over medium heat, stirring occasionally, until the sugar dissolves. Cover and boil for a few minutes without stirring. Remove from the heat, add the tablespoon of plain moonshine, and mix. Using a spoon, quickly drop 2-inch discs of the mixture on top of the crushed candy in the mold or on the mat. Place a lollipop stick into the center of each disc, and twist the stick until it's completely covered in the mixture. Let the pops cool, and store overnight in an airtight container.

STORING

You obviously need to store any moonshine that you don't drink right away. For short-term storage, a plastic container will do the trick—in a cool, dark place away from heat. If you'll be hanging onto that hooch long-term—a year or more—use glass because plastic might taint the taste over time. Glass is also a safer option for storage and is heat-resistant.

Whether you go with glass or plastic, find a safe spot away from heat and sunlight. Consider keeping it in the freezer or refrigerator if you like it cold or for chilly drinks. You might even want to store some in a cool, dark space, some in the refrigerator, and some in the freezer so you can whip up a cocktail at any temperature you like. Do what makes your moonshine taste best!

TIP

To identify your moonshine easily, apply chalkboard paint to the front of the jar, let dry, and label the jar with chalk. Tie a strip of burlap and black fabric around the lid for a little extra flair.

Chalk

LABELED JARS

Don't store your expertly mixed hooch in an ordinary jar. Add one of these labels to customize your craft. Copy or scan-and-print these pages onto a blank sticker-sheet and trim the label out.

MOONSHINE
ALMOND
FLAVORING

MOONSHINE
APRICOT
FLAVORING

MOONSHINE
CINNAMON
FLAVORING

MOONSHINE
COCONUT
FLAVORING

MOONSHINE
COFFEE
FLAVORING

MOONSHINE
CRANBERRY
FLAVORING

MOONSHINE
GINGER
FLAVORING

MOONSHINE
JALAPEÑO
FLAVORING

MOONSHINE
RASPBERRY
FLAVORING

MOONSHINE
ROOT BEER
FLAVORING

MOONSHINE
SWEET TEA
FLAVORING

MOONSHINE
VANILLA
FLAVORING

MIXING STATION

Set a table with assorted mixers, several jars of flavored moonshine, and sodas. Prepare freshly cut lemon and lime wedges, fill a bucket with ice, and arrange glassware. Let your guests mix and match different pairings and craft their own concoctions.

TIP

Set out a cup filled with cinnamon sticks for your guests to use as stirrers or garnishes.

TASTER TOWER

Help your guests get their shine on with a Taster Tower that features several flavors for simple taste tests. Just mix the flavors, then set them out with some small glasses on a handmade or store-bought stand.

MOONSHINE KIT

If you're sharing the gift of 'shine with friends, show them how fun mixing it can be. This kit takes minutes to assemble and might get you invited over for a few drinks! Fill a small gift basket with a jar of plain moonshine and the ingredients the recipient will need to flavor it: jalapeño, ginger, mint, etc. Type or write out a mini recipe card and slip it inside.

COCKTAIL KIT

Another fun gift for your family and friends is a cocktail kit. Any alcohol enthusiast will love one of these. Fill a gift basket with a jar of flavored moonshine and the ingredients the recipient will need to make two cocktails. Include two glasses for serving the drink. Type or write out the recipe and slip it inside the basket or one of the glasses.

MOONSHINE MIXOLOGY

SHINE ON

MOONSHINE FESTIVALS

Enjoying moonshine doesn't have to end at home. After you hook your friends on hooch, check out some of these moonshine festivals around the country where you can drink spirits with good, like-minded company.

NEW STRAITSVILLE MOONSHINE FESTIVAL

This celebration kicks off every Memorial Day weekend in the rolling hills of southeastern Ohio. Go for the parades, moonshine still display, local history museum, flea market vendors, moonshine burgers, moonshine pie, moonshine doggies, carnival rides, games, and more. For more information, visit www.facebook.com/Moonshine-Festival-274679112574192.

ETOWAH MOONSHINE FESTIVAL

Savannah Oaks Winery in Tennessee throws this summertime event. Take part in two days of music, crafts, spirits, and beer. Visit www.etowahmoonshinefestival.com for more information.

THE MOONSHINERS BALL

Enjoy some white lightning while listening to indie rock, bluegrass, and Americana at a beautiful outdoor arena in the Appalachian hills in Berea, Kentucky. Festivalgoers celebrate local art, music, and poetry while dancing and drinking under clear, star-lit skies. For more information, visit www.themoonshinersball.com.

THE VIRGINIA MOONSHINE FESTIVAL

The shine is strong in at this one. Come November they have loads of distillers, food vendors, and beer and wine suppliers, plus live bluegrass and country bands. Visit http://vamoonshinefestival.com for more information.

MOUNTAIN MOONSHINE FESTIVAL

With forty-six years under its belt, this all-ages festival is well known and well respected. Each October, 'shine-lovers flock to Dawson, Georgia, to see the origins of NASCAR racing, sample moonshine, watch the car show, listen to live entertainment, and shop for specialty crafts. Visit kareforkids.org/mountain-moonshine-festival.html for more information.

INDEX

Note: Page numbers in *italics* indicate recipes.

ABOUT THE AUTHOR

Cory Straub developed an interest in wine and moonshine at a young age when he watched his grandpa make it. Cory started making his own wine after high school and grew interested in moonshine once it became commercially available. He has been perfecting his grandfather's moonshine recipes for twenty-five years. He began with a five-gallon bucket, experimented with commercial kits, and even constructed his own distillation equipment. He lives in Ogden, Utah.

ACKNOWLEDGMENTS

Matt Shay - Art Director
Brandy Shay - Project Management/Drink Stylist
Cynthia Levens - Co-Author/Editor
Toni J Studios - Photography
Chelsi Johnston - Projects/Food Stylist